Female
Impersonation

by

Avery Willard

FIRST EDITION

Published by Regiment Publications
P. O. Box 247
Grand Central Station
New York, N. Y. 10017

2

FOREWORD

An Agnewism would imply that: "When you've seen one female impersonator, you've seen them all." That is not true. I learned this a few years ago when I was introduced to a popular entertainer, Minette, who was perhaps one of the most interesting personalities I had met in my life. His knowledge of people and life was particularly extensive. He was certainly not the "shallow" person that, frankly, I had expected him to be. Through my association with Minette and the many other impersonators whom I have since met, I have gained a special appreciation of their unusual art: for it truly is art, to those who take it seriously.

I believe I know more female impersonators than most people do, therefore I speak with a certain amount of authority when I say that, as entertainers, they are a serious, sincere, hardworking group, in addition to which, they are 'nice people'.

Compiling the material for this book has been a rewarding experience for me. If it is half as interesting to the reader, it will have been time doubly well spent. I hope, too, that those of you who have entertained the idea of joining this illustrious profession of female mimicry will find some inspiration in these pages.

I want to express my gratitude to those whose cooperation has been invaluable, especially Leslie Marlowe, and B.P., and I hope you like the fruits of your extensive labors.

Too, in a book of this type there will be omissions, due to the endless numbers of people involved in the profession of which we write, some of whom were not able to be reached and others who replied too late to be included, for which we are truly sorry. But then, isn't that what produces revised editions?

I offer, to professionals who share my enthusiasm for female impersonators, whatever data relative to the profession which I have available and which they might like to peruse, including photographs. And those of you who have experience with female mimicry on the legitimate stage or in Hollywood are asked to exchange that information, for possible inclusion in a future tome which will delve into those areas.

Your comments and suggestions, both good and bad, will be appreciated.

Avery Willard
P. O. Box 352
Grand Central Station
New York, N.Y. 10017

3

A HISTORY OF
FEMALE IMPERSONATION

IMPERSONATE: to assume the role of, theatrically, or fraudulently; to mimic.

The filed of impersonation is replete with tales of honest, as well as fraudulent female impersonators, some of whom, due to their associations with kings and dynasties have been recorded in history. Not the least of these are taken from the beginnings of social history, the Age of Sophocles and Pericles, when it was not uncommon for the citizenry to worship a God who embodied both sexes, and who was represented in both male and female attire. Dionysus, in physical and mental characteristics is represented effeminately. In Bacchic festivals in his honor, it was customary for men, in female clothing to mingle with the frolickers. Venus Castina was a Goddess who responded with special sympathy to the yearnings of female souls supposedly locked up in male bodies.

It is known that Herodotus in his travels as a doctor discovered, on the island of Skyth, on the north shores of the black sea, a society of males who were wearing female attire and who were doing women's work. They displayed predominant female characteristics.

Ancient Greek art shows many males wearing female attire. Not the least of these was Hercules, who in female clothing, served his Mistress Omphale.

Caesar and Nero both had their moments. Nero taking particular delight in wearing masks which were modelled to resemble the faces of the Roman women whom he particularly admired. When Nero's wife, Poppea, died, he looked vainly for her successor in all the women he saw. Finally he selected a young boy, Sporus, who underwent a sex change, and whom Nero married.

Caesar lived as a girl, with King Bithynia, and clothed himself in female garb. He had the hair plucked from his soft body, and on occasion, even disported himself as a painted prostitute.

Yes, history gives instance after instance of men admired - even revered - who happily appeared in public in female attire.

Claudius is known to have celebrated the rites of the Egyptian Goddess Isis dressed as a priestess. Paris, that marvelous pride of masculinity appeared in Roman Theatrics impersonating nymphs and goddesses such as Pelopea and Philomela. And there was the comic, Ubicus.

In those days it was considered sport for a man to dress as a woman, and if he gave his all to his role, no one thought any the less of him for it. Rome was famous for it's masculine beauty, and pretty boys who masqueraded as women were much admired by the Roman Senators as well as their wives, who included them in their festivities dressed thusly.

Older Russian societies have considered it a mark of high honor for any family to rear a transvestite son, and on the Dutch Island of Maarken it is the custom to dress boys as girls until they reach the age of seven. In Madagascar and Indochina, males are sometimes brought up as females. Even the American Indian tribes relegated special roles to certain of their young men, who were dressed as women, and who were treated as such.

The lure of female clothing has long held a fascination to men of many occupations. Circus performers were known to have used female impersonators on the high wire and in similar roles because it was felt that the movement of the women's clothing gave a special gracefulness to these acts, thus combining beauty and danger.

France, perhaps because there has been more recorded history, has contributed many stories, some bizarre, to the history of female impersonation.

It has been said that Napoleon Bonaparte possessed one of the most extensive feminine wardrobes in Europe, which he wore. He considered himself a collector and much of what he owned had it's own exotic history, such as the dancing costumes which dated to the Ming Dynasty, the bloomers and furs once owned by a Russian Empress, and the many examples of women's shoes and stockings. Being bi-sexual, Napoleon also had a collection of fur garments for his penis and testicles, which he displayed at appropriate moments.

Though twice married, Philip, Duke of Orleans, son of Louis XIII, dressed as a woman, and busied himself with their hair styles and details of their gowns. He died in 1701, at the age of sixty, still dressed as a handsome dowager.

The Abbe de Choisy, of the Court of Louis XIV, another famous female impersonator, was considered to be one of the most interesting of all history. Though not of royal birth, he was closely associated with the court through his father, the Chancellor to the Duke of Orleans. His mother, of the noble family of Harault, dressed her son, whose real name was Francois Timeleon, as a girl from the time of his birth. He left a book - "Memoirs of Choisy" - in which he discussed his life as a female impersonator, relating instances such as his appearances, in the theatre, as a girl, which deceived

Continued on Page 70   5

SONNE TEAL

A TRIBUTE

Sonne Teal is dead. He was killed several years ago in an airplane accident in Europe where he had gone to live and work.

Before his death we had written Sonne asking permission to do an article about him. It had been more than nine years since we had done his first professional photographs. Since that time, Sonne had had an illustrious career. I met him in 1955 while he was appearing at the 82 Club in New York City. Sonne had come to the "big city" from North Dakota, having migrated there from Canada, with his parents.

The story of Sonne Teal starts with his North Dakota teaching assignments, for a year, in an art institute. It ends with Sonne becomming the rage of the continent and being killed when flying to fulfill an engagement.

While in college, he studied with a modern ballet group, which gave him the background for his later work. Afterward he joined a female impersonation revue, which toured for half a year before coming to New York City. His hobby was 'sewing', thus he always wore the most beautiful gowns where ever he appeared. Shortly after coming to New York, Sonne met and fell in love with Caesar. Caesar's greatest joy was to go walking with Sonne through the vastness of New York. For Sonne it was tiring. For Caesar it was a comfort, for Caesar never took a step. Caesar was probably the most beautiful cat Sonne had ever seen! Thus the love affair!

Roger Stefani, choreographer of the world famous Carrousel, in Paris, saw Sonne's performance at the 82 Club in New York, while he was, himself, making a personal appearance at the Latin Quarter. He immediately offered Sonne a contract to appear with him in Paris. Within one year, Sonne was co-starred at the Carrousel opposite the then rage of Paris, Bambi. As a result, Sonne received his most fabulous contract — an appearance at the Casino de Paris, as one of the featured stars. "Sensations de Paris" ran for two fantastic years.

The rest of the continent clamored to see Sonne. Thus began his tour of Europe, culminating in a trip to North Africa.

At about this time, Jacques Baratier, well-known film director, was casting the starring role in a new film. It would feature a star who would be willing to expose herself. Two famed European actresses turned down the role which left M. Baratier frantic.

Continued on page 9

A friend, however, suggested that he use Sonne Teal — a name unknown to Mr. Baratier. A trip to Brussels was arranged, where Sonne's performance was viewed with delight. M. Baratier still didn't know that Sonne wasn't a female. The contracts were drawn up two weeks later in London, where Sonne was then appearing. Sonne was engaged to play the dual role of 'Marion' and 'The Doll' in the film, "La Poupee" which was first presented at the Berlin Film Festival and was later distributed, with much success, all over the world.

When Sonne sent me the photos which are reproduced with this article, he asked me not to use those older photos which I had originally taken of him, saying:"I like the new, modern Sonne Teal better than the 'old one'". And new and modern he certainly was, for as I sat watching him on the screen in "La Poupee" I found it difficult to believe that this was the same Sonne I had known. Everything about him seemed different — only his eyes looked the same!

Sonne's letter showed that he hadn't changed "inside" where it really counts! He was appearing at the Ches Nous Cabaret in West Berlin, Germany, when he wrote the following letter (in part):

" Dear Avery,

How nice of you to write me after so much time has passed since our last meeting. And how nice of you to think of me for the new book. After nine years away, it is gratifying to know that there are still professional people who remember me, and who think I am of interest to the American public."

Everywhere — the people who knew him, as well as the people who saw him perform — do remember Sonne, with fondness!

SONNE TEAL

MARIO MONTEZ

Mario Montez made his film debut in Jack Smith's "Flaming Creatures" in 1962. Even though he appeared on the screen briefly toward the end of the film as a Spanish dancer, he left a lasting impression. Viewers found it difficult to determine whether the brunette who whirled on the screen with a rose in "her" teeth was a male or a female. Unfortunately, this is the film the police confiscated ; the court˙declared it obscene and banned its showing in New York.

In a period of a few years Mario has become a Super-star in underground films. For underground film maker Ron Rice (now dead) he appeared in "Chum-Lum". Two more films for Jack Smith — "Normal Love" and "The Borrowed Tambourine". Other film appearances include: "Brothel" and "Waiting For Sugar" (For Bill Vehr); "Grapes of Wrath" and "Mid-Summer Night's Dream" (For Charles Ludlam); "Lupe" (For Jose Soltero); "Dirt" (For Piero Heliczer); "Flaming Twenties" and "Gypsy's Ball" (For Ava-Graph).

Mr. Montez made several films for Andy Warhol, in the 1960's, one of which was "The Chelsea Girls." Others include "Dracula," "Harlot" "Hedy," "Camping," "More Milk Yvette" and "The Buffern Pilot."

In Ava-Graph's "Flaming Twenties," he created a variety of roles - flapper, zany chorus girl, Ziegfeld Follies beauty - and in "Gypsy's Ball" he was an evil fortune teller.

He has appeared in two major films: "Candy," and "The Queen."

Mario has a special interest in films, to the point of being star struck, particularly with Maria Montez, who was his film idol - hence his own name. He designs and sews most of the costumes which he wears, and often makes those worn by his fellow actors, making him a well-liked person.

Mario with Charles Ludlam in "Trillby"

Mario with White Pussy

Jack Smith filming Mario in "The Borrowed Tambourine."

Mario in Ava-Graph's "Flaming Twenties."

Mario in "Flaming Creatures"

Mario in Ava-Graph's
"Flaming Twenties"

14

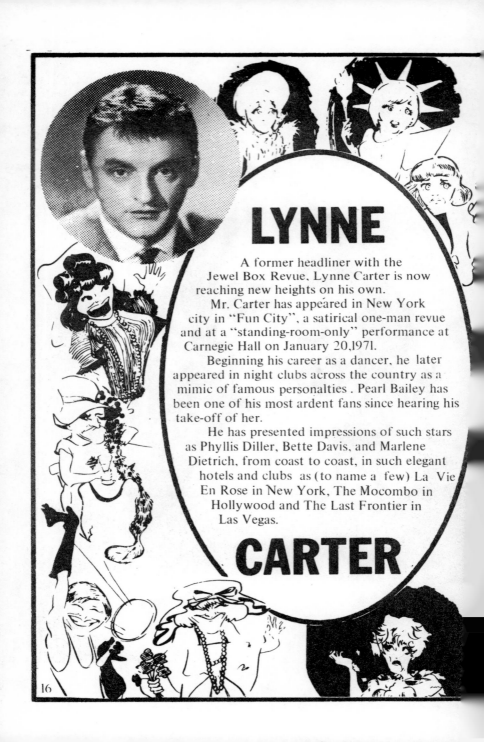

LYNNE

A former headliner with the Jewel Box Revue, Lynne Carter is now reaching new heights on his own.

Mr. Carter has appeared in New York city in "Fun City", a satirical one-man revue and at a "standing-room-only" performance at Carnegie Hall on January 20,1971.

Beginning his career as a dancer, he later appeared in night clubs across the country as a mimic of famous personalties . Pearl Bailey has been one of his most ardent fans since hearing his take-off of her.

He has presented impressions of such stars as Phyllis Diller, Bette Davis, and Marlene Dietrich, from coast to coast, in such elegant hotels and clubs as (to name a few) La Vie En Rose in New York, The Mocombo in Hollywood and The Last Frontier in Las Vegas.

CARTER

Mr. Lynne Carter

MINETTE

WHY BECOME A FEMALE IMPERSONATOR?

How do I tell you why I became a female impersonator? Perhaps I might recall the questions most frequently asked of me by my fans - with the exception of: Baby can I see you after the show? -

1) Most people ask me HOW I first started.

So-o-o. . . I guess my first real professional appearance was made at the age of three, when I appeared on stage with my aunt - who was a "house singer" in a burlesque theatre. I had developed the ability to mimic, and I did impressions of the then popular artists. It wasn't until many years afterward, however, that I switched to drag, after doing a song-and-dance act in vaudeville, and working in night clubs as band vocalist - I was a "crooner!"

Since early childhood my attention was drawn to the feminine mannerisms - so the transition from trousers to dresses came naturally, I would say.

Sometimes, in jest of course, I tell my nightclub inquirers that I switched to drag because I got "too old to pass myself off as a boy any more!" How true!

Boston, in 1948, was "drag wild." Anyone who looked pretty in a dress was assured of employment as an impersonator. I played a one year "return" engagement at the popular College Inn, in 1951. By this time female impersonators were appearing in many of the "straight" shows, too. The public seemed to love us. They actually stood in line, waiting entree to this nuge club.

I am reminded of an article in the December 30th paper. It was written by the (then) Archbishop Cushing, and in it he condemned female impersonation as "the lowest form of animal life." Well, that did it. His power was unquestionable, as a result of which many of the Boston cabarets closed - voluntarily - and New Year's Eve found not a single impersonator working in Boston!

This is mentioned to give the reader an idea of one of the pitfalls that follows this profession. It's not all gold, spangles and laughs.

2) Many people ask me if I feel gratified personally as well as artistically, when working as a female impersonator.

My reply: This art allows me to reveal the "real me," in my best - and most fitting - costume: a pretty dress. I actually believe that I was intended to be a woman - however I wouldn't go through the sex change that others endure, as I think I am fairly well adjusted to my role in life, and don't need it. Actually, I enjoy being different. It makes my act unique, I guess, and I attribute my success to my long years of "basics" in show business.

3) I am frequently asked what I consider my greatest asset in performing.

Other than being a mimic at an early age, I was influenced by the finest artists of the day, including Ruth Etting, Belle Baker, Ethel Waters and Mae West. They convinced me of the importance of developing a style of my own. Also, I know that music has always been important to me. From my very beginnings I was surrounded by the sweet blues, hot jazz and the wail of the torch singers. How could I not be influenced by that?

4) Do I have any advice for impersonator aspirants?

Right now the field is somewhat limited. It just isn't what it was years ago - as recently as the early forties. It takes a tremendous amount of drive and determination to overcome the obstacles that present themselves. And then, once established, there must be a constant effort to improve; not only the act, but one's appearance, what with makeup and hair styles constantly changing. An important factor in any night club appearance is stage lighting. Knowing what the lights do to you can be an asset. I always check the lighting very carefully, wherever I appear, sometimes finding it advantageous to be nice to the light man. Thus I can adjust makeup and be the real "glamour girl" that I set out to be.

An act, incidentally, is never finished. There are constant rehearsals, until the act is so well known that it could be performed in the dark...and who knows, In New York, with the brownouts and blackouts, it might even become necessary to do it!

An exquisite war_robe is, of course, a must, for a femme fatale.

Finally, remember PHOTOGRAPHS! Without good photos to supply to agents and clubs, you'll get no advance publicity. And, let's face it, publicity is what we are looking for in this business...especially if it's GOOD.

And NOW - do you think that YOU have talent? - And persistence? - And enough love of life (combined with guts) to make it? - Then, go to it! and GOOD LUCK! Who knows, maybe we'll be working together some day soon!

Edward Blessington and Minette
in Ava-Graph's
"The Last of the Worthingtons".

Minette
in Ava-Graph's
"Flaming Twenties"

21

LESLIE
MARLOWE

23

Born in Los Angeles, of a family of vaudevillians, Leslie Marlowe has been both a successful female impersonator and a producer. When he saw his first female impersonation show, he knew what his work would be, so he applied for and got a job dancing in a chorus line. Leslie has since had a succession of engagements throughout the country. He embarked upon a mad whirl through Ohio, Pennsylvania, Maryland and other East Coast states, where he enjoyed long runs. Perhaps some of his smartest early successes were in San Francisco, where he appeared at the Beige Room and at Ann's 400 Club.

New York City has had several opportunities to enjoy Leslie's unusual talent, and Greenwich Village hasn't been quite the same since he did his long engagements at the Moroccan Village and the Soiree Club.

It was while in New York City that Leslie met Ed Kaplan, a booking agent, who started Leslie on the road to producing his own female impersonation revues. Through this association, Leslie helped innumerable artists to further their careers. In fact, he originated the showcase for femme mimic talent, which he called, Female Mimics Revue, and which toured successfully.

Leslie's now well-known one-man show became a weekly feature at the Dellwood Hotel, in Cairo, New York, each July and August, while his shows toured elsewhere.

The revue, "Call Us Mister?" which featured a real girl stripper, was produced by and featured Leslie Marlowe. He was also the first female impersonator to appear at Brooklyn's Club Interlude and Sabella's. Leslie has appeared with such personalities as Titanic, Bruno Le Fantastique (half man-half woman act), Baby Martel, G. G. Allen, Chi-Chi Laverne and others. He appeared with the comedy impersonator Karlos, for a three week run at Toronto's Victory Theatre.

The Club Paddock - Davy Jones Locker - Club Flamboo - You name them, Leslie Marlowe has played them. And Leslie is truly leading a fascinating life. When he isn't busily engaged in putting a travelling show together, he can be found under a glamorous spotlight somewhere.

25

CHRIS MOORE

The glamorous Chris Moore made quite a splash into show business just a few years ago.

While appearing with Frank Bennett in New York in the revue, "Follies Mantisque" in the mid sixties, Chris came to the attention of Danny Brown. This led to an engagement with the Jewel Box Revue, with Chris doing a comedy strip and singing in a baritone-soprano voice.

Later, he discovered that he was good at imitating Ethel Merman and created a lot of attention singing selections from "Gypsy". "I sound just like her when I'm in good form", Chris says, with a smile.

Adding to his repertoire, he began doing take-offs on Dietrich and Bette Davis. Another highlight of his act is his "Annie Oakley" impression.

Chris has appeared in clubs and theatres all over the east coast. Even though he is a native of California (San Francisco born), he has never appeared there. "I love New York", Chris says.

Of his many accomplishments, Chris is most proud of what he refers to as his two "Oscars," - his award for the Most Outstanding Performance bestowed upon him at Frankie Quinn's April in Paris Ball, and Lee Brewster's Mardi Gras Ball (1971).

"Don't forget to mention my awards," he says, as he brings them out for all to see.

Before becoming an impersonator, Chris devoted four and one half years to the U. S. Army. He has also travelled all over the world as a merchant seaman, and has lived for one year in the Orient. Quite a background for his art!

"But New York is my home, I love it!" says Chris.

A FORMER HEADLINER

One of the real pioneers of female impersonation had a Broadway Theatre named after him. Born William Dalton, in Newtonville, Massachusetts, Julian Eltinge (as he was known professionally) began his career as a female impersonator at the age of 14, when he played a girl's part in a show presented by the Boston Cadets. He was such a smash hit that the following year the show was written especially to feature his talents.

That was the beginning of a steady rise to fame that reached its culmination in 1910 when the New York theatre was named after him. His fame continued however, until after his retirement. For even though he had 'put aside' his personal appearances, he was constantly being asked to return, and return he did, until almost the day of his death in 1941.

Julian lived in a comfortable apartment on Fifty-seventh Street in New York City, just a stone's throw from Broadway, thus he was always under the influence of the bright lights. He was a star on Broadway at the tender age of twenty!

Two of his big hits on Broadway were: "The Crinoline Girl", at the famous Knickerbocker Theatre and "The Fascinating Widow."

Hollywood beckoned and he went west where he made many films. Among the movies in which Eltinge appeared were: "Countess Charming", "The Clever Mrs. Carfax", "Maid to Order" and "The Widow's Mite"

Perhaps the highlight of his personal life was the "command performance" he gave in London before King Edward VII, at Windsor Castle.

Among the many of the society clubs at which he appeared was the world famous Diamond Horseshoe, operated by Billy Rose (One of the frequent visitors there was Fanny Brice)

It is said that Julian Eltinge went through three fortunes and those who knew him will attest to the fact that he was lavish in his attentions to his many friends, thus assuring himself of being the "honey" in the bee-hive of activity.

Theatre critic Cecil Smith wrote of him; "grace, charm and good manner, dominated his actions, and whole families came to his eminently decent shows."

JULIAN ELTINGE

Julian Eltinge and his Mother

Scene from "Countess Charming" – Paramount Film – 1917

ADRIAN

In the years prior to Fidel Castro's take-over, Havana nightlife was very gay. One of the bigger attractions to tourists (as well as to the Cubans) was a fabulous show called, "Midnight In Paris," at the MonMartre Club. The shows highlight was the appearance of a fantastically veiled dancer, who, midst belching smoke and flames, nightly captivated the audiences. Thus did Adrian make his big name in Havana. And this subsequent fame started him on a fabulous trip around the world.

He was only sixteen when Havana first heard of Adrian, and he was appearing in a club of conventional acts. His flame dance act followed, and then he was featured in a television series called, appropriately, "Tropics."

All Havana worried as Castro's movement expanded. One night, during his act, Adrian heard several shots ring out in the room. When the lights came up, three persons lay dead, victims of Castro's underground. That was Adrian's cue to depart.

"Salome and the Dance of the Seven Veils," introduced the Club 82's new season to New Yorkers, in 1958. It was an immediate hit, and Adrian stayed on for four years, delighting audiences who came from all parts of the country and the world to see him. One reason for its success was the fact that Adrian, wanting everything to go perfectly, designed and made his own costume. He discovered a new talent, which he continues to use.

The wax head of John the Baptiste, which he uses in his act, is the same one that Brenda Lewis used in the Metropolitan Opera.

Adrian's act is not the kind that can be ignored, but occasionally a table of "talkers" will disrupt the proceedings, at which Adrian usually directs his act to that table. One group of four women were so engrossed in what they had to say that nothing that Adrian could do seemed to get their attention. At an appropriate moment, however, and uttering

a horrendous shriek, he slid the gory-looking head down onto their table. One of the four keeled over in a dead faint, and a second was seen making a mad dash from the club. The others repaired-shall we say-to the ladies room. . . and none of the four was ever the same, it is believed.

A series of commuter-style appearances between Florida's Gold Coast and New York City, followed, and Adrian had the distinction of being the only female impersonator to appear at a benefit sponsored by June Havoc - which is still being talked about.

Australia intrigues Adrian, as well as Europe, and he is trying to make connections for appearances there.

D.D. GRIFFO

D.D. in Ava-Graph's "If Ads Were True"

AVA-GRAPH MADE ME - A STAR!
by: D.D. GRIFFO

Some years ago, a local organization, of which I was a member, presented me with the task of heading a fund raising campaign. They had already exhausted the conventional methods of fund raising and I found myself at a loss for a new idea. A telephone call, one evening, temporarily put the problem out of my mind, for I heard my friend inviting me to what sounded like a "fun evening". Goodness knows I needed some relaxation! Little did I know, however, what this fun evening would portend!

The invitation was to a special screening of "SPEAKEASY QUEEN" and "FASHIONS OF THE TWENTIES", two films produced by a group known as AVA-GRAPH.

When the screen lit up, my initial reaction was one of amusement. However the amusement turned to fascination in a moment as I became absorbed by the realism of the presentation. The most amazing feature of the film was the fact that the "actresses" weren't women at all — but MEN! The films were replete with original period gowns and appropriate sets. As I sat there listening to the enthusiastic reactions of the viewers, I was suddenly struck with the realization that here was the answer to my earlier problem. I would arrange for a booking of these films!

Immediately after the showing, I met AVA-GRAPH'S creator and producer, AVERY WILLARD, a tall young man whose eyes shown as he discussed his film work. His enthusiasm was positivily contagious! Out of this meeting there grew a rewarding association with AVA-GRAPH, and — of all things — my subsequent appearance on the silver screen as a female mimic!

Initially I became AVA-GRAPH'S publicity director (work, you know, before glamour!) At this time I was appearing in an Off-Broadway presentation of "The Man Who Came To Dinner". Avery saw me in the role of the elderly butler (I was all of 26!) and thought I would be perfect for a part in his forthcoming film, "The Dead Sister's Secret". I was thrilled to be offered the featured part of

D.D. in Ava-Graph's "Variety" (left) and as Bertie Hornsby in
Ava-Graph's "The Dead Sister's Secret" (right)

Bertie Hornsby. This would be the first step up the ladder of success to stardom! The 'first step' was shaky, though, because some of the members of the cast thought that my appearance was odd — for the role — I was six feet five inches tall and weighed 140 pounds; too tall and too thin! At the first screening, months later, they discovered that my acting far outshone the vital statistics; proving that Avery Willard knew what he was doing.

Until the time that shooting began I had not seen my costume complete. Well! Did I have a good laugh! In addition to a gray wig and glasses worn off the nose, it consisted of a gingham skirt (yards and yards of fabric were used), a blouse with high lace cuffs, an old-fashioned bonnet, an apron, long black stockings, and TENNIS SHOES!

After the cast and crew had stopped laughing I learned that I was the mother of two grown daughters (in the film, that is)! Then the director handed me my script and announced that most of my scenes would be in the can in a few days. Little did I know then the number of hours and sweat until my role was completed in "The Dead Sister's Secret" — but don't get me wrong — it was worth every minute of it!

AVA-GRAPH

Formed in 1956, by Avery Willard, the author of FEMALE IMPERSONATION, AVA-GRAPH became one of the newer underground film groups, which dedicated itself to recording of female impersonation in film. Running the gamut from full-length to documentary-type films, the group soon made a name for itself, at first showing in a small New York City loft, and then moving to progressively larger quarters. Its founder, who was also its cinematographer, not to mention costumer, lighting man, director and sometimes-script writer, collected an arsenal of magnificent gowns bought from defunct Broadway shows and theatrical costume houses, which equalled-if not surpassed- any then assembled for use in impersonation films.

When the Shubert organization, in 1955, sold its world-famed costume collection, which contained gowns worn by some of the most famous female stage personalities in history, Avery Willard, having AVA-GRAPH in mind, was one of the largest purchasers.

The list of films that follows, gives an indication of the scope of the group's efforts. Many have been shown to women's groups, who seem especially to enjoy female impersonation, from coast to coast, and they are still available from the author of FEMALE IMPERSONATION.

1. "SPEAKEASY QUEEN," introduced MINETTE and featured BILLY RICHARDS, TOM LEWIS, JERRY NUNES, GEORGE SCHROEDERS and KIVA, in a story of a nightclub girl of the Twenties who meets a handsome swain. A color film, with a special musical score by Pianola. Running time: 30 minutes.

2. "FASHIONS OF THE TWENTIES" also featured MINNETTE, BILLY RICHARDS' TOM LEWIS' GEORGE SCHROEDERS, and TERRY LANE, ALEXIS MARTEL and DAVID. Here the original fashions and music of the Twenties was shown with commentary. In color. Running time: 30 minutes. 1958.

3. "THE LAST OF THE WORTHINGTONS." A story about a London vampire, set in the Gay 90's, with an original score composed and played by HAL SYKES. The film, which runs 1 hour and ten minutes, and is in black and white, stars MINETTE, HARVEY LEE and TA-TA. Also featured are TOM LEWIS, EDWARD BLESSINGTON, FREDERICK FRINK, ARTHUR GEIGER and CONNIE CARTER. 1961.

FILMS

4. "MAGIC MUSIC HALL" features KWAN NUYEN, MINETTE, BILLY RICHARDS, TA-TA, DORAN DeWINTERS, BOB DAVIS, FRANK MELTON and ALLEN FRANKLIN. A black and white film which runs 15 minutes. 1961.

5. "THE DEAD SISTER'S SECRET" stars MINETTE, VALERIE VELOUR, TA-TA, and features STUART GOODWIN, FREDERICK FRINK, PAULA GINSBERG, D. D. GRIFFO, BUCK ROGERS, APRIL CALHOUN, KWAN NUYEN, JONATHON ·MARK and LEO GENTRY, and is a story about "Lilly Lou," and the foreclosure on the Hornsby Farm. It is complete with vamps and villains the story being by HAL SYKES. In color, the running time is 50 minutes. 1962.

6. "VARIETY" stars MINETTE, D. D. GRIFFO, TA-TA, IRMA LA DOUCE, DOLLY DIMPLE, JACKIE LOVE, ROY QUATTROCCHI, JOHN CRAIG and SULTANA. In color, with the actual voices of well-known personalities. Running tome: 12 minutes. 1963.

7. "IF ADS WERE TRUE," filmed in color in 1963, is Ava-Graph's answer to TV Commercials, featuring MINETTE, D. D. GRIFFO, IRMA LA DOUCE, FREDERICK FRINK, JACKIE LOVE, ROY QUATTROCCHI, ROBERT VAUGHN, DON ASH, VALERIE VELOUR, BRUCE MICHAEL and MARK PETERS. It runs 15 min.

8. "TWO WAYS" features expressive ANGIE SAXON and WAYNE ROBERTS, in a provocative strip-tease, in color, and running 15 minutes. 1964.

9. "SALOME AND THE DANCE OF THE SEVEN VEILS," features ADRIAN, in a 10 minute color film made in 1965.

10. "THE PERILS OF PAULETTE," is a tour de force for JOLIE DERRIERE in four exciting escapades ala Pearl White. It also features APRIL CALHOUN and SEPTEMBER MORNE, with ROCKY LA RUE, TONY STRONG, ED TAME, DEAN DENNIS, and AL WORTH. This color film runs 30 minutes. 1966.

11. "SKIN AND LEATHER," was an innovation for AVA-GRAPH, being just what it implies. Running 15 minutes, this color film stars CHUCK JASON. 1966.

12. REFLECTIONS," introduced PAUL RITCHARDS, perhaps one of Americas most handsome men, in a panoply of pattern and movement in kaleidoscopic color. Running time of this avant-garde film is 10 minutes. 1966

13. "DREAM BOY," also stars PAUL RITCHARDS in a rhapsodic fantasy, in color. The running time is 20 minutes. 1966.

14. "MY JOHN" Stars: D.D. GRIFFO. Features: FRANK CARR, AL WORTH and CHUCK JASON. This is Ava-Graph's interpretation of Warhol's "My Hustler". In pulsating color. Running time: 15 min. 1966.

15. "AVA-GRAPH GOES TO A DOUBLE WEDDING" An unusual documentary of a real-life, he-he wedding. In color. Running time: 12 min. 1966

16. "LEATHER NARCISSUS" Stars FERNANDO. A psychedelic effect film which tells the fascinating story, in modern fantasy, of the well-known Narcissus myth. In color. Running time: 40 min. 1967.

17. "FOUNTAINS" Features: ROBERT MICHAEL, GREG NORTH, TONY RICHARDS, SANDY TAYLOR and PAUL RICHARDS. Five famous New York fountains like you've never seen them before, spurting, splashing and caressing beautiful male nudes. In sexy color. Running time: 20 min. 1968

18. "FLAMING TWENTIES" Stars: MINETTE, VALERIE VELOUR, TA-TA, D.D. GRIFFO, MARIO MONTEZ and DAWN CHANNELLE. Features underground film makers and stars JACK SMITH, CHARLES LUDLUM and BILL VEHR. This is a satirical film, compromising a collection of vignettes of the entertainment personalties who were famous during the "Roaring Twenties". Included is a take-off of the Ziegfeld Follies girl-parade, which features Ava-Graph's own pretty girls. Original music of the twenties. In stunning color. Running time: 45 min. 1968.

19. "RUGGED MEN" Features: BOB ROY, JOHN PETROFF, KURT SANDOR, TONY STRONG, THE ORR and FRANK PACE. Six rough and ready men strip for your pleasure. In virile color. Running time: 20 min. 1969.

20. "CAMP BURLESQUE" Stars PUDGY ROBERTS. Satirical short, featuring Pudgy's famous night club act. In color. Running time: 6 min. 1969.

21. "THE GYPSY'S BALL" Stars MARIO MONTEZ, WAYNE ROBERTS and BILL WOOD. Adventures of Lilly Lonely a wicked gypsy and a mischievous boy. In color. Running time: 20 min. 1969.

It is interesting to note that, in 1966, the AVA-GRAPH work went from femininity to virility. This was a result of a group decision to do so, and to use impersonators as vamps where needed.

More recently the filming included numbers of nude shots, but done in so exotic a way as s to be classified as Art.

Ava-Graph's
"PERILS OF PAULETTE"

Scenes From Ava-Graph Films

G.G. ALLEN

G. G. Allen first appeared as a female impersonator at the age of fourteen, at a club in New Orleans. When the club owner learned his real age, G. G. was sent back home to Mobile, Alabama.

His next engagement, professionally, that is, was at the Carnival Lounge in Pittsburgh, where he remained for four years, working in various clubs.

In 1950 he joined the Babe Baker Ha Ha Revue, which played engagements in Detroit, Cleveland and Milwaukee.

Misfortune beset G. G. when both of his legs were broken in an automobile accident. In recovering, G. G. studied singing and even dancing. It was the dancing that really strengthened his legs. He studied with Oreste Sergievsky and with the Monte Carlo School of Ballet. He was so proficient that he became a dance instructor for a while. But the call of the "yonder" beckoned, and G. G. took to the road, touring the Eastern part of the States as an impersonator, appearing with name groups.

The Moroccan Village, in New York's Greenwich Village, was quite THE place for female impersonators at one time, and it was there that G. G. made his initial appearance. Following that he went to the famous 82 Club, also in the Village. Philadelphia then beckoned, and while there, G. G. was asked if he would like to join the famed Jewel Box Revue. His answer was immediate, "Yes!." - And G. G. became one of the hits of the Revue, which toured the country.

1959 found the Jewel Box Revue at Loews State Theater on Times Square (that was when that theater vied with the Palace for its vaudeville shows) and G. G. practically stole the show with his impersonations of Bette Davis, Helen Morgan, Tallulah Bankhead and Judy Garland. He also did a fantastic Can Can dancer stint. G. G's audiences invariably applauded his Judy Garland impersonation, and even G. G. liked it the most of all his routines

One reviewer at Loews State recounted hearing a heated debate between a man and woman sitting behind him, regarding G. G's gender. which they couldn't bring to a conclusion.

A successful engagement at Brown's Hotel, in Monticello, followed his appearance at the Shubert in Washington, D. C. And then the 82 Club, in New York, signed him again for the time he had before he started his famous two year appearance at the Jewel Box Club in Kansas City.

Tragedy struck G. G. again. He lost his voice, and his doctor told him not to "talk" for a year. Eight months later, G. G. suddenly realized that the doctor had said not to "talk," and so he tried to sing. . . and it worked!

With the return of his singing voice, his talking voice also re-appeared, and so he was at it again, moving to Wichita for a job, and then on to Tulsa, where he appeared at a popular club. He liked Oklahoma and Tulsa so much that he opened his own bar there - which later became one of the big-time clubs, entertaining, amongst its customers, the - as he called them, "rough and roudy" Osage Indians, - who, as a result of owning oil wells, were big-time spenders.

After a while, Tulsa began to cramp G. G's style, and then-suddenly - in one day, he decided to go back to the big city, New York, and he was gone by the end of that day!

G.G's sights are set on Europe, where he hopes to treat the natives to his personal brand of entertainment.

A perfectionist, G. G. Allen is at heart a very serious person. Anyone who has seen him perform will be aware of the professional quality of his work. He has achieved stature as a female impersonator, although still young.

ROBIN
ROGERS

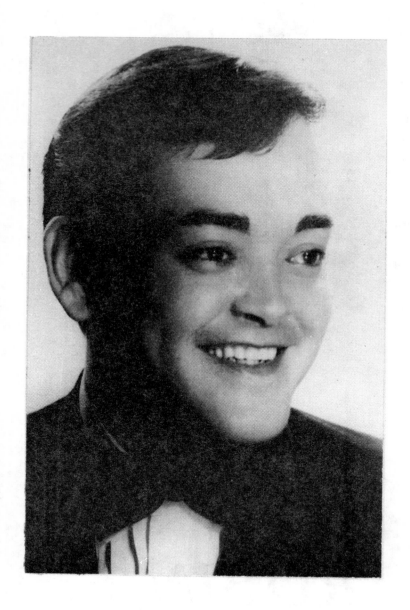

It has been an exciting show! The chorus of "Luck Be A Lady", can be heard ringing through-out the darkened club. And now, having completed "her" mezzo soprano solo, Robin Rogers steps to the rear of the stage. Her handsome young partner, Darrell Stewart, steps into the spotlight to sing the verse. As he does so Robin turns his back to the audience. That, in case you didn't know it, is class! He is about to steal the spotlight from his partner! The two have just completed an evening of fabulous entertaining, the latter part of which they devoted to their impression of Jeannette McDonald and Nelson Eddy singing the old favorites. The audience loved it — every bit of it!

And now, Darrel Stewart is rejoined by — but, what's this? Who is the young MAN, wearing a tux and flashing a broad smile, singing along with Darrel? Where is Robin Rogers?

Now, don't get nervous! Nothing has happened to Robin Rogers. As a matter of fact, Robin is right there on stage doing his -- er, her - hocus-pocus "sex-switch" ... and right in front of the audience too! No, there are no doctors involved in this switch. This one is for "appearances" only. It's part of the fantastic finale of the Jewel Box Revue, in which Robin Rogers removes his female attire (with his back to the audience) and displays the male garb he has been wearing underneath. Truly, it's a great act!

In 1960, Robin met Danny Brown, who immediately put him under personal contract. Before that, Robin, who had no formal voice training, had sung in the US Navy Choir. That was the beginning of his traveling life; for the choir gave a series of church concerts throughout the country, including one at Convention Hall in Atlantic City and a special concert for Cardinal Spellman at the Astor Hotel in New York City.

After serving his country, Robin, who has a range of three and a half to four octaves, became a singing waiter in a New York club. It was there that a friend heard him and was so impressed that he arranged the introduction to Danny Brown. Danny was half of the producing team of the famed Jewel Box Revue. Although Robin had no knowledge of female impersonating, he put himself in Danny's hands and six months later he joined the revue for a short run.

As is so often the case, show business takes over and one's plans are forced to change. Robin was so successful that de developed a solo act with which he toured all the famous clubs of the USA, including the El Captain and the Music Box Theatre in Hollywood. At the Music Box he was part of a two hour female impersonator revue. The critics were amazed with his uncanny impression of Helen Morgan and they predicted a brilliant future for him. The Riverside Hotel, in Reno, Nevado, had an opportunity to cheer his solo performance shortly afterward and he was launched on a career of impersonation.

Female impersonation is not the eventual aim of this rising young personality. Robin has his eye on television and films, in which he hopes to do a male presentation, using all he has learned thus far, as springboard. He plans also to do some recordings.

One of his severest critics is his wife, who is a junior executive in an auto accessory firm.

In New York City, at the close of the Jewel Box Revue run, Robin spoke candidly about his career.

"I think female impersonation is a real art. It's one of the most difficult areas of show business. People come to be shown and it takes a well-timed and perfectly presented routine to win them over. If it is properly pursued, it is just as rewarding for the artist as it is for the audience."

We know — for we had just heard him sing... as a young lady and as a handsome young man, with a thrilling baritone voice.

STORME
DE LARVERIE

CALL HIM "MISS"!

To begin at the beginning is the best way. And when that way includes a Christmas Eve Baby, you really have something going for you!

After having seen her on the stage many times, in the revue TWENTY FIVE MEN AND A GIRL, I was fascinated to learn that Storme De Larverie was, indeed, just such a Christmas Eve baby.

She never knew her real parents (a white father and a negro mother), having been reared by foster parents in New Orleans, where she was born in 1920.

When she isn't appearing on stage as a male mimic, Storme might be found doing a number of other things, such as, cutting her own hair, modelling (for artists or photographers), laying tile flooring, writing poetry or magazine articles, collecting good luck statuettes (elephants with upraised trunks), or reading, reading, reading.

Storme (pronounced Storm-y) has had an adventuresome life. In early childhood she became an accomplished equestrienne, and her New Orleans environment provided her with excellent training for her future calling as a vocalist. More recently she has been active in an air-conditioning business and she has done some interior decorating, having laid an entire floor of tile with one hand! It seems she had crushed two fingers of the other hand when a heavy fire door closed on them.

Her singing career began in 1940, travelling with bands that appeared throughout the country. At one time she had a band of her own, in which she was featured vocalist, and which appeared for three years at the Royal American.

It was not until 1955 that she worked in male attire for the very first time.. and she loved it. Combined with her sultry voice she was a "good-looking boy" according to a member of the orchestra who had to show her how to tie a bow-tie.

Storme now always dresses like a man - which is undoubtedly why she is so convincing on stage. She has twenty pairs of boots - in which she is very interested. Her collection of men's suits is impressive. It is a better selection than can be found in many men's closets.

In her male attire, Storme is constantly taken as a man...or is it "mistaken?" As a result, she has collected some interesting stories about her escapades. Once such concerns her plight in trying to locate a cab, on the day she was to see her Avery Willard photo proofs. Storme has a thing about punctuality, and so she was going out of her mind because no cabs were in sight. Finally, after what seemed an interminable delay, one pulled up. Just as Storme opened the door, she heard a voice say, "Thank you, Son," and a little old lady swept into the cab. With a straight face, Storme muttered, "Yes, Mam," and began looking for another cab.

Again, one early morning, Storme was on the subway. Two young toughs boarded the car and attempted to mug a sleeping passenger - the only other occupant. Storme got up and protested, and just then the train stopped. One of the toughs exited in a hurry, because he didn't like the looks of this guy in the leather jacket and boots. The other one, however, swaggered over to Storme saying, "Say, Buddy, wadda ya buttin' in fer?" Calmly, Storme explained that what he was doing was wrong, at which the tough pulled a knife and said, "What if I use this on you."

Storme, still calm, put her hands into her leather jacket pockets and replied, "Well, then, I guess I'D just have to kill you!"

"So long, Buddy!" the punk shouted, as he raced for the next car, and out the door at the next stop.

Storme breathed a sigh of relief - because her pockets were empty.

It is amusing to Storme to see the numbers of people who think of her as "one of the boys," simply because she is appearing - as a boy - in a revue with boys who masquerade as girls. Recently, when she was asked whether she preferred to be called "he" or "she," her reply was, "Whatever makes YOU feel the most comfortable."

In her writings about life and work, she has this to say, "Women and men think pretty much the same. I hear both sides of the story - for I am one and I mimic the other."

ANGIE
SAXON

Angie Saxon is one of those extremely warm-hearted out-going persons, who create a favorable impressions on almost everyone they meet. It is said that Angie never knowingly said a harsh word about anyone, so how could he be any other way? He is a hard worker, striving constantly to improve his work.

His work? — Oh, yes! Angie Saxon is a female impersonator. But not just "a" female impersonator, for Angie has the unusual distinction of possessing a fully developed female bust. Angie's physical capaciousness, like Topsy, "just growed!" - and without the aid of hormones.

It is reported that the Army doctor who examined Angie for the draft referred to him as "one of nature's miracles," adding, "nature was also generous!"

Born in St. Louis, of a Greek Mother and an English Father, Angie combined both physical genders in his unusual facial expression, which has been described as "quixotic." He capitalized upon this expression by becoming a female impersonator, which he worked at for six years in New York City, and at various clubs in the Eastern States. The Top Hat and the Four Seasons, in Long Island, and the well-known Harbour Club, on Staten Island, all know his work.

Doing a film for Ava-Graph, in New York, Angie found himself stranded in a New Jersey bus station without any immediate transportation, and he was due to start shooting within the hour. A stranger offered him a lift, because he said he couldn't bear the sight of a young lady - marooned! Angie, in full makeup, said nothing - only played his part well, when suddenly the car was involved in an accident. He was shook-up but not injured.

In the car immediately following, were six husky college boys. When they saw this trim, chic 'doll' in a gold lame dress, standing alongside the road, they immediately offered assistance, and so Angie found "herself" crushed between those admiring hunks of masculinity, who played for her favor all the way into the big city! - and who never did know that "she" was really a "he."

That ride brought out the best in Angie, as the Ava-Graph film "TWO WAYS" attests. He - "she" - is billed as, "QUEEN of Striptease."

CALL HER "MISTER"!

BARBETTE

Austin, Texas is the home of Vander Barbette, a man who once held spellbound countless thousands of people the world over with his high wire act that was second to none, and which French critics hailed for it's beauty and delicacy.

Jean Cocteau, the French poet, novelist, dramatist and film-maker, once wrote a now well-known essay about Barbette in which he said, "He walked tightrope high above the audience without falling, above incongruity, death, bad taste, indecency, "indignation." Cocteau marvelled at the care which Barbette took in applying make-up which changed him from a man into a girl. "Jekyll is Hyde!" said Cocteau when Barbette's wig was finally in place, and his fingers ringed.

Barbette was born Vander Clyde, at Round Rock, Texas in 1904. He became interested in wire-walking, when still in school, he saw his first circus and loved it. He devoted countless hours to practising on his Mother's galvanized-iron clothesline strung across the backyard.

Shortly after graduating from high school, he amswered a "Billboard" ad, placed by one of the Alfaretta Sisters — world famous aerialists — who needed a partner for a trapeze and swinging-ring act, to replace her sister who had died. She asked him if he would appear in women's clothes, since the act appeared more dangerous and dramatic if it appeared that a woman was doing it. He said yes, starting him on a career that was to bring him the plaudits of millions.

He went on to work with a number of circus acts, including one in which, wearing huge butterfly wings, he hung by his teeth on a revolving apparatus with two other people. He learned everything to be known about trapeze artistry.

Barbette then began to work on his own act which eventually made him famous. For his first entrance he wore an elaborate ball gown and an ostrich-feather hat. On the stage, along with the conventional stretched wire, a trapeze, and hanging rings, was a sofa covered with a white bearskin, on which Barbette did a kind of a strip-tease, removing his long evening gown and revealing a tou-tou, which he wore while he swung out over the heads of his audience on a trapeze, hanging first by one foot, then the other, pretending to fall, all the while wearing a face that looked like an

Continued on page 79   69

A HISTORY OF FEMALE IMPERSONATION

Continued from page 5

everyone. He later became an Abbey and was given a seat opposite the pulpit. At the age of thrity-two, he gave up female attire, and became the Ambassador to Louis XIV in Siam.

Later, he returned to his previous role-playing, and under the name of Madame Sancy, he married a Monsieur de Maulny. Monsieur de Maulny, however, was , in truth, Mademoiselle Charlotte, who dressed as a male! And so they were married, he as the bride, and she as the groom. The marriage did not work out, though, and they were divorced, Charlotte still a virgin. Said the Abbey, "I never attacked her honor, because I was much too engrossed with my own beauty."

He next lived with an actress, who also dressed in male attire. Their union produced a lovely little girl.

The Abbe de Choisy died at the age of eighty-one, then wearing male dress, since he felt that he no longer looked well in female clothing.

A contemporary of the Abbe de Choisy, was the Abbe d' Entragues, who belonged to the Balzac family, and whose brother married the half-sister of the King's mistress, Louise delaValliere. Because his mother wanted a girl, he was raised as one in every detail. When he later became an abbey, he wore the garb of his calling during the day, but reverted to feminine clothing at night. It is said that he wanted so very much to have soft white hands that he slept with his arms tied above his head, believeing that would keep them that way. He lived to be eighty.

One of the more sensational tales about a man-woman, is that of the Chevalier D' Eon, who made his debut into history as a rival of Madame de Pompadour, becoming a pretty mistress to King Louis XV. When the King discovered the deception he took a fancy to the young lad and took him into his service. What's that about one good turn deserving another?

In the service of His Majesty, D 'Eon, disgusied as a young woman, went on secret missions. In 1755 he went to Russia, disguised as the niece of the King's accredited agent, the Chevalier Douglas. He was able to gather much valuable information, but the details of how this was done will not be entered into here.

Two faces of The Chevalier D'Eon.

So successful was D 'Eon that it became a popular diversion among the French people to wager bets on him with strangers who saw him for the first time as to his sex. At the time of his death in 1728, at the age of eighty-two, D'Eon was examined by a Dr. Copeland, to determine which gender he really belonged to and the following statement was issued: "I certify by these presents that I inspected the body of Chevalier D'Eon in the presence of M. Adair, M. Wilson and Father Elisee (first surgeon to Louis XVIII), and have found the male organs perfectly formed."

Modern times are not without parallels.

During World War I, a Bristish aviation ace, Major Yeates Brown, who worked as a spy for England, lived as a German governess in Constandtinople. It is said, also, that some German fighter pilots shot down in England during the war were discovered wearing girl's panties and bras. Even the Russian infantry loved silk, and in a 1944 filed order prohibited the wearing of anything other than panties and bras! Of course, although it wasn't disclosed until after his death, even Kaiser Wilhelm of Germany loved silk, often wearing lavender underpants and slips.

Two other Europeans well-known for their drag proclivities were Cardinal Montego of Spain, who dressed his choir boys as girls (he is reported to have been bi-sexual), and Aranka Gyvgeny, who appeared as a woman at the State Theatre of Budapest for twenty-three years without the public knowing of the deception.

Continued on page 92

71

John E. Reed
HOLLYWOOD

RAY BOURBON

Ray Bourbon was born in the 1890's on a ranch situated at the Mexican-U.S. border. He admitted being a borderline case ever after.

In an era when using a four letter word got a person jailed, Ray teased the law with his risque songs -"ditties" they were called then - which barely skirted legalities. He suffered the indignities of many arrests, for ridiculous reasons however. One such, on the West Coast, was for a supposedly "obscene performance" in which he - shades of Lenny Bruce! - pantomimed the use of toilet paper, but he won his case and established a precedent for the future.

Ray Bourbon has always been Big-Time, appearing in the finest night clubs all over the world. His appearances at New York's famous Blue Angel and La Vie Parisienne night spots, where he convulsed audiences with his comic impressions of buxom hussies, or as a washerwoman - his favorite act - complete with bucket and mop, are still remembered. When he appeared in the costume of a street evangelist, shaking a tambourine and singing, "We are Sisters of Charity," there wasn't a dry eye in the house.

He was one of the very first performers who dared to make "dirty records," and collectors zealously guard those early 78's, which, though they were considered extremely risque then, are mild by comparison to what the 1970's offers. Nevertheless, Ray's hilarious double entendre became the rage of the smart entertainment world. "AROUND THE WORLD IN 80 WAYS," the title of one of his ten LP albums, gives an inkling of their content.

His fame extended to the continent, where he gave a command performance for King Edward, at Belvedere Castle. He also did a special performance for Generalissimo Franco, in Spain, during the Occupation of the Forties, with Josephine Baker and her famous Paris Folies troupe, in which he was headlined.

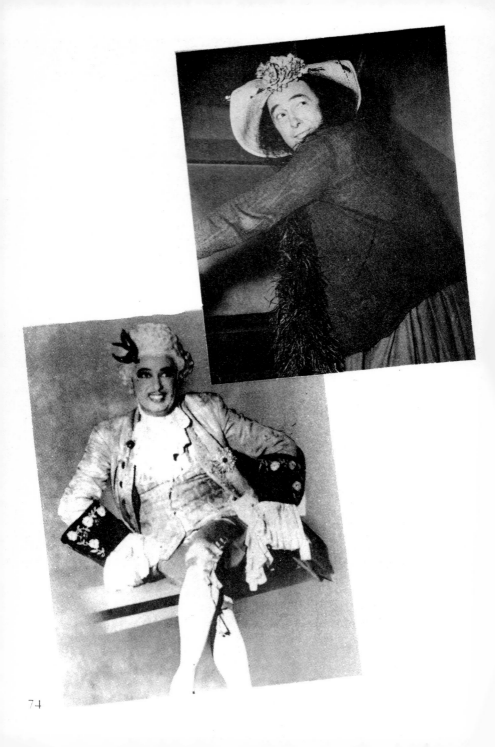

Ray Bourbon got his start in London, while in school, and where his early urge to "act" was fulfilled. Fate cast him in the role of a saucy little Miss in a London stage production, and when everyone told him how pretty he looked - he was hooked! He went on to the Music Halls and an array of little entertainment clubs.

The beginning of the silent film era took Ray to Hollywood, working as an extra, or stand-in to numerous movie greats, such as Clara Bow, Rudolph Valentino, Douglas Fairbanks, and Pola Negri. He was in Miss Negri's first film, "Bella Donna," in which he played a buck-toothed flower vendress, and-later in the film- an arab spy, disguised as a camel driver. With Valentino, he appeared in "The Four Horsemen of The Apocalypse," "The Sheik," "Blood and Sand" and "Son of the Sheik."

RAY'S LAUGH WELL-KNOWN

Ray's trademark was a high-pitched whinny of a laugh, which, once heard, was not easily forgotten.

In 1923, and using his real name, Ramon Icarez (although there is a most interesting tale about THAT, too!), he performed a breath-taking fire dance at the opening of the Los Angeles Coliseum, which stole the show from such as the Theodore Kosloff Dancers, May McAvoy and Dick Strange, who were also on the bill.

Anyone familiar with San Francisco's gay night life, knows that Finnochio's was the high spot of any night out-in the 1930's. Ray was one of the big headliners there. That was the era of the famous - and some infamous - female impersonators, who were so popular that they were featured in the Ziegfeld Follies and in George White's Scandals, and who were the toast of Broadway. Names such as Julian Eltinge, Jackie Maye, Francis Renault, Karyl Norman and Carol Davis, were spoken with hushed wonder, for - like the flappers of the Twenties - they were a sight to behold in their expensive gowns, flashy jewels and overdone style.

Yes - Ray Bourbon was an important part of this milieu. He wowed the customers with his fabulous gowns, although he usually made fun of what he wore. And he almost always came on near the end of his show wearing a messy housedress, a gnarled wig, white saddle shoes and stockings hanging awry. The audience didn't recognize him. He came on stage without fanfare, carrying his bucket and mop, and

RAY & MAE in
"Catherine Was Great"

RAY BOURBON
and MAE WEST

tydied up under the feet of the dancers. It was only after he had caused - and taken - a few pratfalls that they caught on...and then pandemonium reigned!

Ray met Mae West at this time and they became friends. He also opened a club of his own outside of Hollywood, which became a celebrity hangout. Bing Crosby and Bob Hope are reported to have often spoken, on their radio shows, of having been "at Bourbon's."

Offers poured in from clubs everywhere, and so Ray, with a house trailer, a jalopy, fourteen dogs (his "kids," he called them, for he loved his animals), and his entourage, began a series of cross-country pilgrimages, which were broken only by his appearances with Mae West, from 1945 to 1947, in "Catherine Was Great," at New York's Shubert Theatre, followed by a three year tour as Bowery Rose in "Diamond Lil."

For one engagement, a club manager, seeing the advance photographs of Ray - in drag - thought that he was a woman, and so he billed him as R-A-E, a name which Ray used on and off. He put the female name to good use in 1956 when his press agent sent out a release advising that Ray had taken the "switch" and had had his sex changed from he to her. Later, this was proved to be quite untrue.

INTERNATIONALLY KNOWN

Shanghai, Paris, Rome, Cairo...you name the city...Ray was known there.

His club dates went on through the 1950's and in the mid-sixties, travelling through the heat of Texas, Ray's car caught fire and burned. His beloved dogs, in the trailer, were saved by a passing farmer who sprayed the trailer with crop spray, preventing the fire from spreading. Ray left his beloved pets in the care of a pet shop, and continued his tour.

Ray was known to be a soft touch. As a result his finances dwindled as he grew older. Even the dogs remained "unpawned" for three years, although Ray did his best to send money for their care. Even that became a trickle, eventually, and the pet shop owner sold Ray's "kids."

In 1968, at the age of seventy-five and still going strong at the Jewel Box, in Kansas City, Ray was arrested for allegedly master-minding the murder of the pet shop owner. Ray protested his innocence, saying that he certainly would not want dead the only man who could help him regain custody of his pets. One would have to know Ray to understand his tremendous -almost fanatic - love for his dogs.

The State of Texas tried him, found him guilty, and sentenced him to 99 years in prison!

The details of the case were bizarre. There were many irregularities charged by Ray's court-appointed attorney, who filed an appeal.

The appeal was never heard.

Ray Bourbon passed away on July 20th, the victim of a heart attack, complicated by a severe leukemia.

In passing judgment on Ray Bourbon, those who knew him - Yes, even those who only knew him from his stage appearances - will remember not his last frightening years, but rather, the more than fifty - count them FIFTY! - years that he devoted to making us laugh, which he did beautifully.

In his record album "Hollywood Expose," Ray did one number called, "My Petty-gree," which he authored. These are his final lines:

"I've known the wits,
I've known the bores,
I've known the good girls,
And the - - OTHERS!
Though this will never put my name
In the Hall of Fame,
Still I've been around just enough,
To know a few who are BIG stuff!

So time and time alone will tell,
Some day I'll see you all in Hell.
A cheer will rise, and they'll all say:
'Hooray! Hooray! Here comes Ray!

Yes all you guys and all you funks,
(And I'll skip right by you campy funks)
When I'm old and gray - and eighty-seven,
(My God, Mary! She's twice that old now!)
I will have earned my place - in Heaven."

BARBETTE

Continued from page 69

enamelled doll under a blonde wig. The surprise element of his act came at the end, after several curtain calls, when he removed his wig, revealing his masculinity. At that moment he also adopted all the expected masculine mannerisms, flexing his muscles, swelling his chest, strutting like an athlete, leaving his audiences amazed, dumbfounded, and sometimes, embarrassed.

The William Morris Agency sent Barbette to England in 1923, where he was immensely successful. Following this they arranged for him to do his act in Paris. It was to Paris that Barbette related and the Parisians took him to heart. He often wondered if his name, sounding French, made them love him more. Paris became his second home and he made many return engagements to the Alhambra, the Empire, the Moulin Rouge and the Medrano Circus.

Frequently he would take his act to such cities as Berlin, Copenhagen, Madrid, Warsaw, or Barcelona, traveling with "twenty-eight trunks, a maid, and a maid to help the maid," as he put it.

Now in his sixties, very trim (perhaps delicate-looking) and walking with an erect, stiff gait, the result of a crippling affliction of the bones and joints, which along with pneumonia, he contracted after a particularly strenous performance at Loews State Theatre in New York in 1938, which brought his sensational career to a sudden end, Barbette devotes his energies to teaching at his own school for trapezists, in Austin, Texas, where he tries to give young acrobats some faint idea of what a refined act can be.

KARYL NORMAN

Karyl Norman had two remarkable voices, one baritone, and the other soprano, and he was able to switch between th e m at will. This is undoubtedly what made his act unique, and what always got him a standing ovation wherever he appeared.

He was born in 1897. His parentage is a mystery, for he had the high-yellow appearance of a creole, which is why he came to be known as the Creole Fashion Plate. It is said that his ancestry was a combination of French and Italian, however.

In 1925, Variety said of his act, "He does a reverse Kitty Doner, (a male impersonator), without sex-switching, jumping from a male to female falsetto with the agility of a Flatbush commuter changing trollies."

Norman's best work was done in vaudeville, where he sang and made popular such songs as, "Beside a Babbling Brook," "Nobody Loves Me," and - dressed as an Indian - "Immigration Rose." Between his numbers he would appear in overalls and blue denims, carrying a straw hat, and singing, "I Wonder Who." Actually, these male numbers were not "between" for they constituted a part of his act. The audience, however, was frequently perplexed by his quick changes.

Karyl Norman tried his hand at legit drama, in "Lady Do," and "That's My Boy," the latter of which did not get any closer to Broadway than Baltimore, and the first of which was considered a smash flop.

Karyl's last appearance was in 1947 at the Ha-Ha Club, in Hollywood, Florida. He was only fifty years old when he passed away, that year.

Cordially
"Karyl Norman"
The Creole Fashion Plate

BERT SAVOY

Bert Savoy owed his great success as a female impersonator to Jimmy Russell, of the Russell Brothers team, famous for its Irish Servant Girls routine. Until the day that Bert and Jimmy Russel met, Bert had been doing a somewhat mediocre impersonation act in the northwest wilds of the untamed west, as well as in Alaska. Jimmy took Bert under his guidance and shaping, culling, adding, and generally re-working him, soon mad a real pro out of him. During this period, Bert met vaudevillian Jay Brennan, whom he added to his act. With his black tie, straw hat and cane, Jay was a perfect straight man to Bert, who dressed in exaggerated female attire. Where the fashionable hats of the day might sport one or two feathers, Bert wore a virtual waterfall of plumes. He caricatured the glamorous woman by overdoing everything, her mannerisms as well as her fashions.

With Bert Savoy, fashion became camp, and camp became the style-if not the rage.

In their nightclub act, Bert and Jay introduced a character called, Margie, who, though unseen, became famous. Whenever vaudevillians got together, the name Margie immediately started a conversation about Bert and Jay. Bert included her in the many Broadway revues in which he appeared: "Miss 1917," and "The Greenwich Follies of 1920," and also of '22.

According to famous showman John Murray Anderson, Bert Savoy had a paunch and was virtually bald at the height of his career, but these facts always disappeared the moment he stepped onto a stage. A metamorphosis took place!

While at Long Beach, one sunny day, Bert and a friend were caught in a sudden, severe rainstorm. On a high point of land offering no shelter, they huddled under a blanket watching the jagged streaks of lightning coming closer and closer. Then, in a blinding flash, the world ended for both of them.

Show business was truly stunned by the sudden demise of Bert Savoy, and although Jay Brennan tried to go on with the act, with another impersonator, it just wasn't the same, and he brought his career to a close.

FRANCIS

One of the mourners at the funeral of Bert Savoy, was a contemporary of Bert's, Francis Renault, famous in his own way for the fantastic extravaganzas he staged, always with himself featured. Francis brought out the best in his vaudeville turns, using elaborate props of urns, pillars, swagged draperies, and such, plus colorful backdrops (cycloramas), staircases, feathers, and what-have-you.

The real triumph of Renault, though, was his amazing falsetto singing voice, which he used to great aplomb.

Francis Renault got an early start, initially in an act done by Catherine Purnell, in Rhode Island. He then went on with his career, appearing with Gus Edwards as Sunbonnet Sue. Eddie Cantor and George Jessel used him in their shows, and then, using the name Auriema. The Shuberts suggested the name Francis Renault, which he adopted in the early 1900's.

JULIUS Eltinge was the then rage of showbusiness, and was appearing on Broadway in a show with Harry Lauder, famous Irish vocalist. The Lauder show went on the road, and replaced Eltinge with Renault.

Francis worked hard on his voice, developing it into a sweet soprano, which mystified and delighted audiences. Some of the songs he became well-known for, were, "My Hero," "Ah Sweet Mystery of Life," and "The Dress My Mother Wore." He also mimicked Eva Tanguay's "I Don't Care," which was one of the most popular songs of the period.

The Shubert's "Passing Show" on Broadway, starred Fred Allen, among others. Francis was featured in it, wearing a gown which cost one thousand dollars, a goodly sum for that era. Naturally, the name of the number in which he appeared was called "The Diamond Girl."

London and Paris acclaimed Renault. Archibald Haddon, of the Empire News (in 1924) called Renault, "a soprano of convincing quality."

Back in the U.S., Francis opened his own spot, the Club Renault, in Atlantic City, which he operated for several years. Renault, incidentally, introduced Joe Penner (remember: Ya wanna buy a duck?) to the entertainment world, and Joe went on to become a big name in radio.

In 1950, Francis Renault returned to Broadway, garnering praise for his work at the Palace Theatre. Then followed a series of Carnegie Recital Hall concerts, in which he used other acts. His voice was no longer what it used to be, but his stage presence more than made up for it. He continued with these concerts until the year he died, 1956.

RENAULT

Anyone who saw Francis Renault on the street, walking his dogs near the Diplomat Hotel, where he lived, could only have been amazed at his appearance. He looked like an aging truck driver! - Which tells you how remarkable he truly was.

IMPERSONATION IN THE MOVIES

Readers who have seen the films listed here will undoubtedly remember the female impersonations of the stars shown. It is not unusual for Hollywood to employ female impersonation in a film which might otherwise be a dud. How's your memory?

LIONEL BARRYMORE in "The Devil Doll"
LON CHANEY in "The Unholy Three"
CARY GRANT in "I Was A Male War Bride"
BURT LANCASTER in "The List of Adrian Messenger"
JERRY LEWIS in "At War With the Army"
HARVEY LEMBECK in "Stalag 17"
BILLY DEWOLFE ib "Blue Skies"
RITZ BROTHERs
RITZ BROTHERS in "Argentine Nights" (as the Andrews Sisters)
RED SKELTON in "Bathing Beauty"
MICKEY ROONEY in "Babes on Broadway" (as Carmen Miranda)
CHARLIE RUGGLES in "Charley's Aunt"
JACK BENNY in "Charley's Aunt"
RAY BOLGER in "Where's Charley?"
TONY PERKINS in "Psycho"
JACK LEMMON in "Some Like it Hot"
TONY CURTIS in "Some Like it Hot"
FATTY ARBUCKLE in "Miss Fatty's Seaside Lovers"
SIDNEY CHAPLIN (Charlie's brother) in "Charley's Aunt"
BILLY GILBERT in "Ali Baba"
BING CROSBY in "Dixie"
RICARDO MONTALBAN in "Sayonara"
JOHN HUBBARD in "Turnabout"
CHARLES HAWTREY in "Carry on Nurse"
JACK LEMMON in "Pepe"
SPANKY and ALFALFA in one of their Our Gang series.
CHARLIE CHAPLIN in "A Woman"
LAUREL and HARDY in "TWICE TWO"
GEORGE MONTGOMERY in "Ten Gentlemen From West Point"
BOB HOPE in "The Lemon Drop Kid"
GEORGE SANDERS in "The Kremlin Letter"
YUL BRYNNER in "The Magic Christian"
HELMUT BERGER in "The Damned"
PAUL NEWMAN in "WUSA"
LEE J. COBB in "In Like Flint"
JOHN HANSEN in "The Christine Jorgensen Story"
PAUL LYNDE in "The Glass Bottom Boat"

JEREMY STOCKWELL in "The Secret of Dinah East"

FRANKIE AVALON in "Ski Party"
DWAYNE HICKMAN in "Ski Party"
MILTON BERLE
WALLACE BEERY in "SWeedie" films (1914-15)
GILBERT SARONY in "AN Old Maid In Drawing Room"
FATTY ARBUCKLE in "The Waiter's Ball"
FRITZ SCHADE in "Love, Loot and Crash"
BILLY REEVES in "A Ready-Made-Maid"
HANK MANN in "Herman Hero"
STAN LAUREL in "That's My Wife"
GLENN TRYON in "Madame Sans Jane"
BILLY WEST in "Ship Ahoy"
WILLIAM POWEL in "Love Crazy"
TONY RANDALL in "Seven Faces of Dr. Lao"
Male Impersonation
GLORIA SWANSON in "Danger Giri"
ZAZU PITTS in "Red Noses"

On the blank page, at the end of this book, add your own recollected movies to this list. It can be quite a game!

TONY RANDALL as Medusa in "Seven Faces of Dr. Lao"   87

WILLIAM POWEL in "Love Crazy"

JACK BENNY

JL LYNDE
in

e Glass
tom Boat''

89

SIR LAURENCE OLIVIER (left) and KENNETH MORE,
two of Britain's renowned thespians, step out of character
and into female attire to appear in a charity show in London.

UGO TOGNAZZI

SIR
ALEC
GUINNESS
in
"Wise Child"

91

A HISTORY OF FEMALE IMPERSONATION

Continued from page 71

Female impersonation has been, and still is, common in the United States. It is the practice for the Princeton Triangle Club to present a yearly revue in which the female parts are portrayed by male students. Halsey Hills, a Dartmouth football hero of the twenties, was a female impersonator in their annual dramatic presentation. Also, in the twenties, Harry Cahill, an interpreter with the Chicago Opera Company, donned singer Hazel Eden's clothing, during a train trip, and tried to romance William Beck, the company baritone. The deception worked for a while, with everyone giggling about it's success. When the ruse was discovered, at which time Beck punched Cahill in the jaw. Rudolph Valentino was a judge at a beauty contest in Lowell, Massachusetts, which was thrown into an outrage upon discovering that one of the female "beauties" was actually a man!

A University of Michigan student, Lionel Ames, appearing in the play, "Cotton Stockings Never Made a Man Look Twice", got the kind of rave notices for his female impersonation that Julian Eltinge would have beenvied. Ames's photos appeared virtually everywhere, accompied by the story that his "pretty legs" had been insured for $25,000.

Drag — drag — drag! What is there about getting into drag that brings out the different man?Athlete Phillip Holmes appeared in drag in the Princeton Triangle production, "Napoleon Passes", for which he, too, drew raves. And Alabama Auburn College senior, Emmett Goldman, won the title "Queen of the May", over three genuine female contestants!

It is whispered that the husbands of these famous women liked to cross-dress, Dolly Madison, Mrs. Sigmund Freud, and the Empress Eugenie of France. So it would appear that there is a fascination to donning women's clothing that knows no class barriers.

Hollywood certainly has contributed its share to the art of female impersonation. Jackie Coogan appeared as a little girl in "A Dog of Flanders", one of his early films, and famour comic Chic Sale included a middle-aged femme Village character in his act. Billy de Wolfe is well-known for his portrayals of demure misses in a number of films and on the stage.

Recently, television has produced several stars who are perhaps better known for their drag appearances than anything else. Flip Wilson's Geraldine always gets huge laughs, as does Charlie Weaver's femme mimicry, and everyone if familiar with Jonathan Winter's Maude Fricket and the old lady on the motorcycle.

Vaudeville, both in America and abroad, has, of course, used female impersonators since the first performer trod the boards. It is well-known that Shakespeare used all-male casts, making famous such names as Nathan field and Richard Robinson.

A favorite "heroine" of the Restoration Stage, in England, was Edward Kynaston, a grandson (or possibly a great-grandson) of Shakespeare's sister Joan. He became well-known for his portrayals of females. Britisher Nokes, famous for his drag comedy roles, was a particular favorite of Charles ll. Harry Lauder used the selnder Grffin Twins, who did acrobatics while dressed as girls - just as did Barbette did many years later.

Would a story about impersonators be complete without some mention of Mmle. de Maupin, fighting her famous duels, or Maude Adams re-enacting Peter Pan, or Sarah Bernhardt as Hamlet? — all male impersonations. More recently, Judith Anderson attempted a version of Hamlet, which a critic described as looking more like Israel's Golda Meir than a man!

The list of names that should be included in a book of this kind is almost endless, but certainly such personalities as Jackie Maye, Laurie Knight, Chunga Ochoa, Toni Midnight and Leverne Cummings ought to be mentioned. And T.C. Jones has a special niche in more contemporary times, having appeared in Leonard Sillman's New Faces Revue and made a big splash. There is also Jan Britton, Dale Roberts, Bobby Johnson and the ever graceful Harvey Lee.

The list expands ro include Kit Russell, Sandy Rogers, Nicky Gallucci, Gita Gilmore, half-man-half woman act, Bruno le Fantastique, and hilarious, clown-faced femme mimic, Pudgy Roberts.

A glance shows us that the professional names adopted by female impersonators were an important part of their presentation, becoming virtually a part of their stage personalities, which they donned and doffed at will. Names such as Titanic, Ricky Renee, Chi Chi LaVerne, Rene Del Rio, Billy Kamp, and Candy Darling are all campily suggestive.

Continued on page 95

BILLY AUSTIN

Continued from page 93

Who could forget Billy Austin, a featured comic of the famous Jewel Box Revue, or Doddie Daniels Kim August, Brandy Alexander, Ty Bennett, Frankie Bennett, or the one-name impersonators Bambi and Coccinelle? Or old-timer Art West, who appearing as an aging dowager in green face (yes, he actually used green make-up which was superb!) convulsed Cleveland for a long run in 1941?

Phil Black, Harlem's famous impressario has contributed much to the female impersonator scene, and he continues to present spectaculars at least once a year, which are most successful. Frankie Quinn gives successful drag balls.

The world of female impersonation is at present watching a rising star, Charles Pierce, who is now making waves across the U.S. with a new act, as well as Danny La Rue, currently the rage of London.

Yes, they must all share in the glory, for they have all contributed to it, by giving of their time, effort and talent. Without their talent, the names in this book would never have attained sufficient status to be known and remembered in this mad, wonderful, dragulous world of female impersonation!